NO MORE FLOATING BOATS

Move Your Ship – Start Your Journey to a Better You!

Sean C. Gooden, Sr.

TABLE OF CONTENTS

Foreword 3

A Note from the Author................................5

CHAPTER 1 Quiet Desperation 8

CHAPTER 2 Procrastination 12

CHAPTER 3 Don't Listen...................................16

CHAPTER 4 Relationships 20

CHAPTER 5 Inner Peace...................................24

CHAPTER 6 No Time for Time 29

CHAPTER 7 Overcoming Fear 33

CHAPTER 8 Weathering the Storm.................37

CHAPTER 9 If It's Possible, Then It's Real.......42

CHAPTER 10 Don't Give Up! 45

CHAPTER 11 Get to Know Your Bag 48

CHAPTER 12 Consistency................................51

The last CHAPTER Move Your Ship!...................54

Now, Move Your Ship!.......................................55

The information you are about to read in this book is based on powerful and undeniable universal truths that have saved many lives, including that of the author. I repeat. The techniques in this book are real and POWERFUL. Do not read this short book if you are unprepared to take a meaningful and unvarnished look at YOU. Likewise you should not read this short book if you are already your best self and have no use for growth or course correction.

You **should** read this book, however, if you are seeking a way, a method by which you can engineer the <u>best</u> you. If you know there is something you should be doing, but you are unsure of the steps you should take to begin and maintain your journey...then this book is for you. If you have started your journey towards your destiny and are sure of the steps, but you feel stalled out...then this book is for you. While this is not a religious text, spiritual concepts are included.

People are struggling to find a grip; to get ahold of things. This could be you. It could be any of us. So, use this information for your most selfish benefit and gain. Use it to push yourself, your mission, and your family forward. Be unafraid.

Use it as a reference. Read it and come back and read it again. Hopefully, you gain greater insight into self, and motivation for your wealth with each time. Now, pack your bags and get your ship together. Your destiny is calling and we're going on this journey!

"You would rather find purpose, than a job or a career. Purpose crosses disciplines. Purpose is an essential element of you. It is the reason you are on the planet at this particular time in history. Your very existence is wrapped up in the things you are here to fulfill. Whatever you choose for a career path, remember that the struggles along the way are only meant to shape you for your purpose.

When I dared to challenge the system that would relegate us to victims and stereotypes with no clear historical backgrounds, ...no hopes or talents. When I questioned that method of portrayal, a different path opened up for me. The path to MY destiny.

When God has something for you, it doesn't matter who stands against it."

-- Chadwick Boseman (1976-2020), The Black Panther
Addressing Howard University's 150th Commencement in 2018

Foreword
by Dr. Joseph Schaefer, Ph.D., Neuroscience

Throughout my life I have been absolutely drawn to stories and movies that tell the struggle, drama, and glory of personal transformation. Movies compress these magical journeys into a mere 120 minutes or less. And my favorite version of this archetypal story is when the main character's future transforms within a single crucial moment or event.

The mythical tale of the hero's journey is itself a metaphor for our inner struggle of transformation. In this book, Sean has shared the details of his struggle and laid the trail of breadcrumbs to mark the path he used to escape the darkness. The seeds for life transformation can be planted in a single event, but transformation itself takes an excruciatingly long time. Instead of it happening within the length of your favorite two-hour movie, it instead takes decades in the real world.

The great inspirational writer Keith Miller once told me that the way you reach everyone is by telling the very specific details of your own life struggle. He said that everyone will hear their own story when you do this. I have known Sean for 20 years and in his book he shares a very personal story of his own struggle and reinvention. His story connects with each of us as we reconnect with our own dreams. We recognize the years when we left our path, and the re-emergence from darkness into the light. His lessons are very clear and the steps are laid out for all to benefit.

---- Dr. Joseph Schaefer, Ph.D. and 8th degree black belt

"Very much of what's artistic is people's very creative and inventive ways out of impossible situations. They get out of these internal, life situations, and they show us a path...they make a trail, when they do this thing, this daring daylight escape. When we see this, it looks like art."

Paraphrased from

James Taylor 1992, Squibnocket

A Note from the Author...

Let me first thank you for purchasing **No More Floating Boats**©. As I complete the editing of this book with the help of some wonderful scholars, including my Mother (the first female African-American news anchor in Austin, Texas), the world is in the midst of the Coronavirus pandemic. Originally completed in November of 2019, the concepts included here are growing evermore necessary. I struggled with putting these words on paper. I wasn't sure if I was supposed to be the one telling anyone anything. Yet, this message kept trying to break free from my mind, body and soul. I decided to stop fighting against it and go with it. So, vamonos con estos!

The proceeds from this book will be used in three ways. First, it will go towards completion of my undergraduate degree. I started at Morehouse College (Atlanta, GA) in 1989 full of vigor and expectation of finishing, but only completed 2 years. It was my first taste of "failure." I hope one of the lessons you pick up from this book, if not any other, is to never, never give up...regardless of how many times you think you have "failed" or whom may have given up on you. Your life is not a reality tv show. Like storms at sea, things sometime happen that are out of our control. That's not what is important, though. What **is** important, is how you respond; how many times you get up after you have fallen down. I am currently enrolled at Huston-Tillotson University in my hometown of Austin, Texas where I will graduate with a degree in Business Management in 2022.

Secondly, proceeds will go towards the acquisition of a dedicated baking facility for my gourmet cookie company, GoodenSweet Cookies (goodensweetcookies.com), so that we can employ the community and the traditionally unemployable, and mentor youth in business and baking arts.

Lastly, this book will benefit my family, those that came before me and those whom have transitioned in my lifetime. I dedicate this work to my 4 children (Orreon, Sean, Jr., Jaiden, and Etienne), 1 grandchild that's here (Xyliana) and those not yet here, my mother (Brenda), father (Donald), brothers (Anthony, Chris, and Kentae), and my many aunts, uncles and cousins. I love you all dearly. A special shout out goes to my friends around the country and the world.

This work is hard-hitting and direct. It has a humorous undertone, but the subject matter is deadly serious. I originally completed the book in November of 2019, but I was scared to put it out. We'll get to that, but if you live on planet earth, you know that was pre-Covid. Now, as we are forced to adapt to living in the era of Covid-19, we have become more physically sedentary than we have been as a society in a long time. This has a decidedly adverse impact on our mental and spiritual states of being, in addition to all of the grieving we are doing as a nation. Because of that, the techniques that are included here take on a heightened urgency and significance. We are worried about so many things. We're having to cope with so many circumstances we never could have predicted. It's so much to deal with. How do you handle them all? You can't just sit there. That isn't the answer. You can't let them overwhelm you (the hardest part). And you have to figure out how to get there from here. Cool, but where is there?

Don't worry! You can do it. This book can help you! You can chart your best course forward and start moving that direction today!! I hope you choose to do just that by implementing some or all of the techniques you will soon observe. So again, I say...thank you and read on!

If there's something you feel like you need to do, don't delay. Just do it. Tomorrow isn't promised.

To your health and prosperity,

Sean C. Gooden, Sr.

The author, Sean C. Gooden, Sr., in August 2007, 8 months before the biggest storm of his life would knock him off-course and start a 10 year journey back to his definite purpose.

(Photo: Eric Hurst)

CHAPTER 1
Quiet Desperation

Quiet Desperation

"The mass of men lead lives of quiet desperation."

– Henry David Thoreau

Have you ever taken a cruise? If you haven't yet when it's safe again, you should try to find your way on a cruise ship. It's an exhilarating and cathartic experience. There are all these people who make plans to arrive on-time at the port and board a huge boat which has a definite destination, to be completed in a predetermined amount of time. Last summer (2019) I took a 7-day Caribbean cruise with my mother, Brenda. Just she and I. It was the trip of a lifetime! We departed from Miami and stopped at ports in Nassau, Bahamas, the Cayman Islands, and Turks and Caicos. What an amazing production and memory making trip with my mother. Awesome!

The precision and high level execution required to amass hundreds of staff from servers and chefs to ship crew and captain, all in a clearly coordinated effort to take care of the 24 hour needs of hundreds, if not thousands, of passengers is truly an incredible sight to see. Make no mistake about it, there is a clear plan of action. And it is necessary. The open ocean is beautiful, and also deadly. It gives you an idea of the bigness of things and how small we are in comparison to the wonders of God. I'm glad the captain had a plan. The Atlantic is not a place you want to be stuck. They said if anyone were to fall overboard that a lifesaver would be thrown out. But, get this, the ship will not turn around to come back and get you. In fact, they would then call the Coast Guard and report your coordinates and you would have to wait to be rescued. How does that sound? How long do you think you could survive in the open ocean clinging to a lifesaver and waiting to be rescued?

Most of us are in the same place in life. Stuck in the middle of an ocean of worries and despair, unsure of what to do next. Desperately hoping that somebody has our coordinates and is coming to the rescue. The truth is, it's going to be you that saves yourself, and it's going to take a focus and determination that you may not have allowed yourself to experience.

It is that unavoidable focused effort which leads me to write this book and attempt to communicate a sense of purpose to you, in and for your life.

All too often, we wander through life aimlessly. Imagining great things for ourselves and our loved ones. Wishing against all odds that these things will just come to pass simply because we want them and have asked for it. It's a tenuous hope at best, and we know it. There is no engine set up to drive toward the destination. No plan or map to follow to get you there. No clear sense of purpose to get you through the storms which are sure to come. Inevitably we are disappointed and become disillusioned when this tactic of quiet desperation does not bring forth the desired result.

I should know. I tried this approach for years (decades even), and guess what? It NEVER worked. It NEVER yielded the results I desperately wanted. I mean, if my imagination alone could build things, it would have built many cities, thriving businesses and cultural centers, and more. Yet, no matter how hard I "wished" for these and other things to come into existence, nothing would happen. I wanted to do this. I wanted to do that. I was going nowhere fast. I felt like a boat floating directionless in the water.

Not only was I not getting any measurable results, but I was actually endangering myself and my family. Consider a boat with no itinerary, no route of travel and no engine designed to propel it forward to the necessary destination. Now consider what would happen to the goal you want to achieve if you are that boat. Would you get where you wanted to go? What happens when a storm like Covid-19 comes along? How will you handle the winds of change blowing you off-course? Better yet, how will you know when you arrive at your destination?

It is this quiet desperation which contributes to the ruin of man and woman alike. Hoping that "it will all work out" is <u>not</u> a strategy for success. In fact, it is most certainly a guaranteed request for failure. If you are asking the universe and God for something that you want desperately, and yet you have not committed the requisite energies necessary to meet the size of the request, you are offering conflicting desires that the universe won't work out in your favor. You are actually sending mixed messages to God and the universe. You need a consistent message followed by directed action, to offer up to God (however you may define your higher power). The universe won't respond to a rudderless boat. Yet, if you apply a definite plan to your request and work toward it, the universe has an uncanny way of putting the people and circumstances in place to help you achieve the end goal. Suddenly, solutions are showing up that you never could have imagined. Currents start flowing that fit perfectly with the movement that you have created. It will seem supernatural. Yet, it will **feel** very natural. If this is not yet you, don't worry! While it is your responsibility, it's not your fault. Most people don't plan to fail. They just fail to plan. Don't be this person! You have to decide to act, and then apply your will to that decision. For, if you do not, you will forever be waiting to be rescued.

CHAPTER 2
Procrastination

THINGS
I SHOULD
DO

THINGS I DO
WHEN I AM
PROCRASTINATING

THINGS
I WOULD LIKE
TO DO

Procrastination

"Only put off until tomorrow what you are willing to die having left undone."

– Pablo Picasso

"Bow and begin." As a more than 20-year practitioner of Shaolin-Do Kung Fu and Tai Chi, this is a statement I have heard more times than I can count. It is both a starting bell, as well as a beacon. They are the words we hear from our Grandmaster before our tests begin. My teacher once told me that the significance was far deeper. Simply put, once you bow, you must start and complete what you were planning to do that made you bow. You can't bow and then ignore the action necessary. And of course, you must first bow, or decide to do something. Yet, we wait. We procrastinate. As I'm sure you have heard, time is a finite resource. We will talk more about that in a later chapter, but suffice it to say...once it's gone you cannot get it back. So why do we procrastinate? What is procrastination?

Procrastination is defined as the action of delaying or postponing something. Why do we humans do this? Is there a procrastination gene? Is there a set of circumstances that preconditions us to be procrastinators? The answer is remarkably simple. No.

Procrastination is a personal choice that we each have dominion over. You literally have to decide to put something off and continue doing so. For some, this is for a short period of time and for others, it's indefinite and/or forever. I am of the belief, however, that the things we choose to put off are usually the things we need to get done the most. It's almost always something that's fairly important or hugely important. It is this importance and the sheer weight of the object being considered for delay that makes us back away.

Maybe it's starting or completing your education or a course of study. It could be applying for graduate school or starting a business. Writing that book. Starting that garden. Or how about the dreaded weight loss goal that requires you to change some habits and start eating healthy and working out? Perhaps it's reconciling with a family member. In my experience, these things are often accompanied by a blaring siren that only you can hear, and are choosing to ignore. This is a survival siren trying to alert you to what is best for you. But, again, we ignore it. We find other menial sometimes meaningless pursuits to dull the sound of the siren and give us a sense of comfort as we look the other way. It's avoidance in its purest form.

Fortunately, the need doesn't go away just because we put it off. The urgency is different, though. As you continue to dull and mute the siren, it will seem farther and farther away, blunting the urgency that you felt when it first occurred to you. No less necessary, just more distant because you keep pushing it further and further out into the water. This has a devastating effect on the confidence needed to complete the task at hand; to do the thing you are being asked to do. You really should listen and act on it right away! It is a gift just for you! This is your intuitive voice instinctively working to help you chart your course. It is your internal navigator. Your intuitive voice can shield you from danger and enhance your life, but only if you listen and ACT. There are things right now that you have been wanting to do and know would make your life better, yet you continue to put them off until all the conditions are perfect. You know...the old, "I'll get to it as soon as this happens", or "I'll do that as soon as I do this thing first", and "I can't do it because I don't have enough (money, time, space, etc.)."

The excuses are many and varied...yet all excuses. <u>STOP WAITING FOR EVERYTHING TO BE PERFECT BEFORE YOU START</u>. You will never be able to see around a corner. If you keep moving forward, however, you will turn that corner and many more. Waiting for the perfect conditions to be present before you start working on the plan that was gifted to you and you only, is equivalent to you lying to yourself on a daily basis. The conditions will never be perfect. The siren is giving you an assist to create the conditions that you want. Consider that you would not be happy with someone else lying to you on a daily basis, so why are you doing that to yourself? In order to live your best life, it is an unquestioned imperative that you must bow and begin. My teacher once told me, "There are many routes available, but only one way forward." You must listen to and act on what your intuitive voice is telling you, before it's too late and the ghosts of things undone gather around your death bed to ask why you waited too long. Bow and begin.

CHAPTER 3
Don't Listen

Don't Listen

"Remember always that you not only have the right to be an individual, you have an obligation to be one."

– Eleanor Roosevelt

There is a ton of research available on the effects of negative talk. Debbie Downer. Negative Nancy. Don't-Do-It Darrell. Jim Impossible. It can be negative talk that you hear from people around you like coworkers or good friends. It can be negative talk you hear from people you love the most like your parents, spouse or family members. Some people can't do anything but complain and talk negatively about any and everything. Do you know anyone like this? Well, it can also be negative self-talk that you give to yourself. The research shows that this negative talk can have a severely debilitating effect not just on your outlook for your life and its prospects, but also on your physical and mental health.

According to the Mayo Clinic, there are 4 types of negative self-talk, which I believe can be widened to apply to all negative talk. They are:

1. Filtering – Magnifying the negative aspects of a situation and filtering out all of the positive ones.

2. Personalizing – This is where when something bad happens, you automatically blame yourself.

3. Catastrophisizing – Automatically assuming and anticipating the worst possible outcome.

4. Polarizing – Isolating one's self into a pattern of thought that this can only be happening to you.

Truthfully, I think there are more. Either way, all of this negativity causes damage to your brain, your body, its internal organs and its systems, including cardiovascular, digestive, reproductive and endocrine to name a few. We'll address each system and how it is affected by negative talk in another book. But a cursory search of these systems will make it clear what the effects of negative discourse are (be it from you or someone else) on the body's ability to function at optimal levels.

Don't take my word for it. Read the medical journals on the effects of long-term stress on the mind and body. Chances are you have already heard of or have some knowledge of these conditions.

In fact, you have likely experienced these effects. It could be something you experienced personally, or that you witnessed someone you love going through. You can literally die from negative talk as the worrying ulcerates the stomach lining and contributes to the development of hypertensive disorders and heart disease. The word, "disease", can be broken down to mean 'dis'-'ease' or discomfort. It is a discombobulation. Scrambled eggs. Think: "This is your brain. This is your brain on negativity." It's not worth your attention or time and, in the end, it's dangerous for you.

So, don't listen! When you encounter this kind of activity from yourself or anyone else (which you most likely will or have), you must develop and maintain the ability to mute the noise and remove it from your consideration. Maybe you have to remove yourself from that person or environment. That could be difficult in the case of spouse or parents, but you must find a way to distill the information you should keep, from the negative talk meant to drag you down and make you give up. If, on the other hand, you are the source, you have to change the tape that's playing in your head that keeps telling you that you can't do it. It's a lying imposter. You should not tolerate this imposter or give in to any of its whims.

Almost any situation has a 50/50 outcome probability. In other words, it could be bad, sure. But, it could also be good. Don't assign the outcome only as negative when you don't know. And don't allow others to do it for you because they also don't know. Even the most well-intentioned people will sometimes attempt to convince you that you can't do a certain thing. Maybe out of love because they want to "protect" you from the harm of what they are sure is impending failure; or maybe out of fear because they can't see themselves doing it. I hope you can see the fallacy in both. You must realize that it is not for them to decide. It is your life and God's divine will. Take a controlling interest in your own life. When this negative talk rears its ugly head, don't listen. Keep moving forward. Keep cultivating you!

CHAPTER 4
Relationships

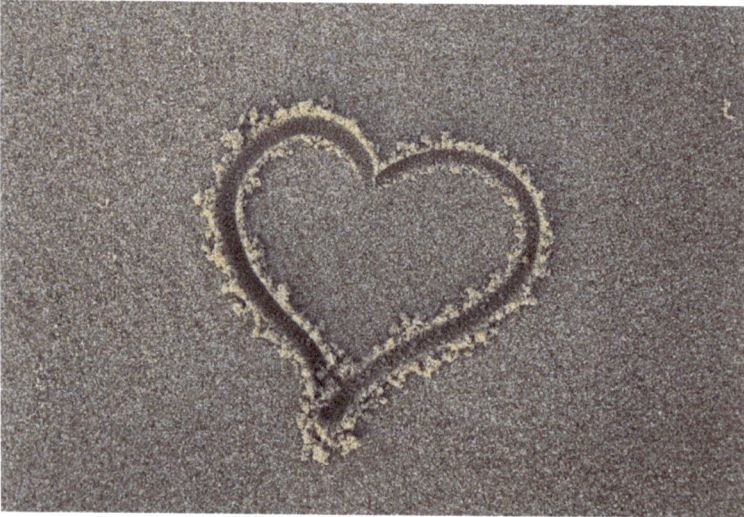

Relationships

Oh boy. Yep. We're going to go there. For the purpose of this chapter, though, when I say relationships, I'm referring to romantic relationships like your girlfriend/boyfriend, spouse or partner. Now, to be honest, we could easily put a chapter in on family relationships because there's lots to unpack there, as well. But, we'll save that for the next edition.

Your girlfriend, boyfriend, spouse or partner should be helping you grow. Period. End of story. He or she should help to propel you forward even if it's only by creating a harmonious and loving environment for you to exist so that you can "man" your ship. This assumes that you are willing to do the same. If this is not happening, you need to reevaluate the value of the relationship. Believe me, I know. I won't say I wasted the years, but I was in a 17-year relationship that was unsuccessful between me and her. Maybe I was too naïve and too willing to wait on conditions that were never going to materialize. Either way, I made the choice to stay and I bare responsibility. Maybe I was projecting what I wanted to be there but clearly wasn't. Ok. So, why stay? Interesting question. Why do people ever stay in situations like that? I'm not sure, but I like to think of it as being unwilling to quit. I'm no quitter. But, where this situation was concerned, I should have been. This person didn't believe in my vision or me. She didn't see how what I was trying to do would benefit us together and that caused major strife between us. It also hamstrung my efforts to put my vision in motion. I'm not saying anything was wrong with her. She just couldn't see my vision for us together. But, together we stayed.

Full disclosure? Perhaps my vision wasn't visible because I wasn't living my truth. Perhaps. In truth, I may have received a different result if I had taken on more responsibility for where I was.

Remember when I said I had wished a lot? It is true that I am responsible for me, and you for you. In a relationship what you really need, though, is somebody who is willing to help you reach your goals and/or define and redefine them, if necessary. You literally cannot have disparate energies, that is energy going in opposite directions, and expect to achieve anything meaningful together.

Speaking in general, sometimes people in your life are there just to feed off of your energy. They like the light that you emit and want to be near it. Yet, they are also threatened by it, and want to keep it from shining as it was meant to shine. Again, it's a personal choice if you stay in a situation like that. Don't play. Be clear about what you are choosing.

I want my life partner to be my teammate and I hers. I thought that if I expressed a desire to combine our lives with love to bind us and a vision of our best future together to guide us, that we would be fine. Sounds good, but all too often that's not how it works in reality, especially if you don't have the right partner.

The bible says you should be evenly yoked. Here's the thing.... It's true whether you read and believe in the bible or not. When choosing or considering the person you will share considerable time with well into the future or for life, it is imperative that you can merge your understandings, not just your loins. Sexual compatibility is easy to achieve. What's hard is spiritual connection. What's hard is operating in a way that together moves you both closer to achieving your God-given purpose. What's more difficult is finding someone who you can vibrate your energies back and forth with, at a high enough level to build and execute the plan.

This isn't just hyperbole, either. In my personal experience, many of the women I have encountered weren't prepared to go with me on this journey. There may be many like this in a lifetime. Oh well. Some will. Some won't. So what? You have possibly experienced something like this in your life, or you may be in the experience right now. I pray for your peace. Just don't lose sight of who you are. You are a unique individual. One of one. You are uniquely gifted with talents, abilities and foresight that no one else has. It is up to you to pull that treasure forward through all the mess, all the distractions and all the noise. Even if it means re-examining your relationship.

Keep things in perspective, though. What I mean is even the most well-meaning person in your life can not do what is for you to do. They can believe in your ability to the utmost and it won't matter if you don't take action for yourself.

"In the end, there doesn't have to be anyone who understands you. There just has to be someone who wants to."

– Robert Brault

CHAPTER 5
Inner Peace

Inner Peace

Before reading this chapter, do this for me: Breathe in slowly through your nose and out through your mouth ten times. --You may decide to stand and raise your arms with each inhale (to shoulder height), and lower them with each exhale, but do it slowly.-- Once you have completed your ten breaths, then start reading this chapter.

Excellent. You have begun to set the conditions for a meditative state that will help you understand the value of the information you are about to receive. Better than knowing its value, however, is applying it. Watch closely.

Your body is nothing if not a series of electrical impulses. These impulses are constantly firing off at predetermined and time determined intervals that coordinate your very being, even when you're sleeping. Every move you make, every step you take is controlled by a line of bio-electrical stimulations that originate from the mind and start a body-wide transfer of information from the medulla oblongata to the tip of your toes. Every breath you take and every thought you make is a coordinated effort from the left and right brain to the rear and frontal cortex. In short, your mind is an immensely powerful computer, and lucky for you and me, it can be programmed to achieve a definite purpose!

How did you feel after your ten breaths? More relaxed? Calm? Possibly light-headed? That is because you were likely taking in more oxygen than you do normally. Don't be alarmed. This is a good thing. The more oxygen you take in, the more oxygenated the red blood cells. The more oxygenated the red blood cells that travel to your internal organs, the better they perform and the better you feel. I don't want to get too technical, but I need to lay a foundation for why you are doing what you're doing and how it will benefit you.

I believe the reason this book reached out to you and asked you to purchase and read it, is because there is an inner turmoil that you are trying to resolve. In order to do that, you need information. Some practical how-to's, for example. I pray, with every fiber in my being, that what you will read and/or have read in this book will feed your soul and give you hope and a reason to move forward.

So, to that inner turmoil. How do we resolve it? Well, I like you have experienced disappointment and great loss. I am not saying that anyone can change that. What **I am** saying is that in order to find your definite purpose, you have to have inner peace. You (inside) have to be still and quiet so that you can listen to your intuitive voice. It's always talking to you. It's not there to annoy you. It's more like a big brother or sister that's trying to look out for you. It's going to tell you things you know are good and right for you, and also things you didn't know. This voice brings you messages from God and your ancestors. It is in this same quietness, and just listening to my intuitive voice that the very idea of this book came to me. In stillness.

Don't be confused. There's a difference between being still so that you can listen, and doing nothing once you've heard. I've had many ideas. Many messages, I assume. Some of them I acted on, but the majority I did not. Who knows what good was in there that may have done something to help others? Les Brown says, "don't let your dreams become the deathbed ghosts that ask why you didn't bring them to the world as God asked of you." Who knows what good YOU can do in the world?!

I have said it already, but these are literally gifts from the ancestors that come directly to you and no one else. You must act on them, but beware ...for **they are up for spiritual grabs if you do not.** There has been at least one other time I had a message as strong as the one that brought this book forward, and that was when I was directed to open my cookie company, GoodenSweet Cookies. You see, my older brother, Anthony, passed away in April of 2008. He was a baker and martial artist just like I am. As a younger brother of 2 ½ years, I mostly followed him and did whatever he did, including martial arts, although he studied a different style. But, he followed me into baking. I started baking and selling chocolate chip cookies from scratch, in high school. Well, fast forward into adulthood and my brother and I were talking about opening a business that would feature his amazing cheesecakes, when he died suddenly from a sparring accident at the tender age of 39. My mom, family and I were devastated and still are. I wanted to do something as a tribute to my brother, and then it hit me like Noah's Ark. "Go bake cookies!" So, I opened my gourmet cookie company in honor of my incredible brother, Anthony, and I am still building it. We spread love one cookie at a time, just like Anthony would have wanted. I still have two incredible younger brothers, Chris and Kentae. I'll get more into the family in the bio, but the point is I heard a message and I have since opened the cookie company to raucous reviews. We want to be the best cookie company the world has seen. There's much to do, and it's work we look forward to! We ship nationwide. Check us out at goodensweetcookies.com .

Regarding **your** message...I'm not a doctor, but I believe you must do something physically exhausting (but safe) to distract the mind from its every day monotony and bring the calm and stillness you need in order to "hear" clearly. Exercise. Workout. Eat cleanly. But, definitely workout at least 2-3 times per week. If nothing else, you will construct a healthier you and that is ONLY good. You can do a number of things and I'll leave that up to you. It could be yoga, dancing, cycling or lifting weights. It could even be walking on a treadmill, but that is what I consider mindless exercise. I wanted something where my mind would have to be engaged, as well as my physiology. After much research, I chose Shaolin-Do Kung Fu and Tai Chi (See www.austinkungfu.com) and have stayed with my teacher of more than two decades, Dr. Joseph Schaefer. I wanted something authentic and mysterious. Kung Fu keeps your body, mind and spirit strong. Tai Chi keeps your body, mind and spirit strong. When you were completing your 10 breaths, the oxygen made you feel better, which makes the mind work better, which opens your chakras and meridians to receive from the atmosphere the energy that is for you. You can use this energy to program your mind to your definite purpose and achieve what others may believe impossible, but you know is actually a gift just to you. Try doing this breathing practice before bed and when you wake up. Take note of what it does for your inner peace. This is the beginning, not the end, of your journey. Become calm so you can be a magnet for your message.

CHAPTER 6
No Time for Time

No Time for Time

"What is time? Time is expiring.... Listen to me. Find your destiny, ...and be destined to get your destination!"

- MJG

Time. There are lots of ways to consider and conceptualize the word. Time can be a moment, over in an instant. It's the way we identify dayparts. It's the calendar. It's birthdays, holidays and special occasions. It's a magazine. Did you know that the study of time is called horology? Physicists and philosophers have long had a robust debate about what time is and how to define its relative existence.

Researchgate.net says:

"Physicists are very clear now. Time is not absolute, despite what common sense tells you and me. Time is relative, and flexible and, according to Einstein, 'the dividing line between past, present, and future is an illusion'. So, reality is ultimately TIMELESS."

ThoughtCo.com says:

"Physicists define time as the progression of events from the past to the present to the future. ...Time can be considered to be the fourth dimension of reality, used to describe events in three-dimensional space. It is not something we can see, touch, or taste, but we can measure its passage."

Wikipedia.com says:

"Time in physics is unambiguously operationally defined as 'what a clock reads'."

There is presentism, eternalism and futurism. Each its own philosophical branch and approach for trying to understand the concept of time. The theories are deep and sometimes mind-boggling. Wonderful to sit and consider, but I want to deal with the more tangible concept of time.

That is, what are you doing with yours? You've no doubt heard people say they don't have time to do...whatever. If you talk to older people, they'll say...time got away from me. But time is what you make of it. It's all about time management. I risk sounding redundant, but it's worth reminding you that each of us gets the same 24hrs in a day. God bless anyone with limitations that may prevent them from using their time in the way others could. Yet, it is still true that from the strongest to the weakest, richest to poorest, most to least educated, English, Spanish or Swahili speaking, we all have the same amount of time to take advantage of each day. Those that realize and employ this time management technique tend to live more fruitful, fulfilling, productive and desirable lives.

There is something good that has been calling to you. Something that you feel a magnetic, almost trance-like connection with and you have been ignoring it in favor of 'another time'. Why? You say to yourself that things would change for the better if you did the thing that has been beating you about the head and neck area. And they surely would, but you have no time for it. We say things like, I could get in shape, if only I had time. Or, I would do it if it wouldn't take so long. It's as if we have no time for time. Do you realize what kind of game you're playing? These are lies. It's flat out not true. God willing, we will see the future together. The truth is there's always something else getting the time you should be devoting to your definite purpose. Candy Crush, some other phone game, or your future? Mind-numbing television or the best you? It's a choice and sacrifice that you <u>must</u> make if you want the success you envision. You are waiting on the right time in the future in order to begin, ...once it gets here. Funny, right? Lies.

I'll bet real money that if you take a sober accounting of how and where you use your time now, you will find an hour or two to use investing in you.

It's going to take some discipline and determination. You're going to have to sacrifice a lazy pleasure that you are currently indulging. Only you know what that is. And now that we are all dealing with stay-at-home orders or something like it, it may have to be an hour away from the tv, computer, or your phone each day so that you can meditate, or take a brisk walk, or get in a good workout. Maybe you don't go to the Zoom happy-hour or no Netflix one night so you can sit quietly and listen to your intuitive voice. Maybe read a book. Consider it self-maintenance. If you think about a high-performance engine that you run nonstop at its highest speed without a break, what's eventually going to happen? You know it. A breakdown. A collapse. Now instead of maintenance, you need a major repair.

Or, you could start carving out a non-negotiable block of time for your own growth and development each day. If you can't start with each day, try 3 - 5 times a week. If you can't do that then make it 2 - 3 times per week. Or, once a week. Whatever it takes, just start now. Declare for you that you will make yourself a priority and be relentless about it. I'm not saying be rude or crude or mean to anyone. I'm saying be good to yourself. I know you may have a family and other responsibilities tugging at your time and you may feel very overwhelmed. It's hard to see the forest for the trees. Trust me and trust your intuition. It will make you better at anything else you're doing or want to do. You need this.

Never forget that your body is the vessel that is carrying you through this journey. The more maintenance you take the time to do, the longer your vessel will transport you. There is always time for that.

CHAPTER 7
Overcoming Fear

Overcoming Fear

The Health/Hope Continuum©, by Sean Gooden, Sr.

(Say it out loud)

Health is Wealth

Wealth is Information

Information leads to Good Business

Good Business brings Better Health

No Hope is Bad Business

Bad Business brings Poor Health

Poor Health leads to Hopelessness

F.E.A.R. = False Evidence Appearing Real.

According to Adam Smith, author of <u>The Bravest You: 5 Steps to Fight Your Biggest Fears, Find Your Passion and Unlock Your Extraordinary Life</u>, the top 10 biggest fears holding you back from success are: 1) Fear of inadequacy, 2) Fear of uncertainty, 3) Fear of failure, 4) Fear of rejection, 5) Fear of missing out, 6) Fear of change, 7) Fear of losing control, 8) Fear of being judged, 9) Fear of something bad happening, and 10) Fear of getting hurt.

It's crippling, this fear. It drags around behind you like a piece of toilet paper on your shoe. It seems to chase you and be waiting on you at the same time. Truthfully, each of these fears have a basis in the human condition. Tony Robbins frequently mentions the 6 needs that we all have. First, the need for certainty. Second, the need for variety. Third, the need for significance. Fourth, the need for love and connection. Fifth, the need for growth. And, sixth, the need for contribution.

You can almost link each of our fears to each of our needs. It's like a self-fulfilling prophecy where we need certainty and are super afraid of uncertainty. So, we end up scared into a paralysis where nothing gets done, thereby guaranteeing uncertainty and the feelings of inadequacy and failure we fear the most. It's a never-ending cycle spiraling downward. Ironic, isn't it?

The fear we feel is based on things that we imagine or anticipate could happen. Let me repeat that. The fear we feel is based on things that we imagine or anticipate could happen. The things we fear don't actually exist, in reality. We literally create an imaginary circumstance in our mind that then dominates and plagues us to the point of freezing us in our tracks, and it hasn't even come to pass! It may not ever come to pass. Yet, in most cases, it stops us from even trying. Goes like this.... Your intuitive voice starts talking to you and gives you a gem. What's the first thing we do? We start thinking about all the reasons why it won't work. We start thinking about who would accept this from you, and what people will think about you. We start imagining our family and friends taking away their validation of us as the person that they know because they can't see it for you. We start thinking about what we could lose if we gave it a shot. And, you're right. It's scary because you can't guarantee the outcome. I can't guarantee you'll be a success if you try, but I can guarantee you won't be successful if you don't. My teacher, Master Joseph Schaefer, 8th Degree Black Belt and PhD in Neuroscience from the University of Texas at Austin, often says, "run toward your fears."

Remember, all situations have a 50/50 outcome probability. Could be bad. Could be good. But you won't know until you try. And, even if you do "fail", you will have learned valuable lessons and gained invaluable insights into yourself that can help move you forward to the next step so you have an opportunity to fail there. In other words, even if you fail, it's not the end. See it as a chance to address and learn from your weaknesses. It is a chance to increase your capabilities and ensure your success in the future. The bible says faith without works is dead. That's true, but this is not about a particular religion. It's about perseverance and undeterred belief. You have to believe in and have confidence in yourself to the point that you never question whether or not you can accomplish your definite purpose, even if it takes more than one attempt.

The mind will accept whatever mandate you give it. It <u>cannot</u> distinguish between a message that is good for you versus one that is detrimental to you. It will act on whatever you feed it, irresponsive of whether or not it's positive or negative. And, it will give you the direct result of that messaging. So, if you feed your mind **positive** messages of success, your mind will be charged to create the conditions that bring that success into reality. Conversely, if you feed your mind **negative** messages of your unavoidable failure and complete inability to see it through, then you will receive that end.

As the saying goes, if you think you can't, you're right! You must continue to run up on your fears like Debo in the movie, *Friday*. You have to get mad at the self-image you hold that sees you as incapable or too scared to try. You have to scare the scared you away, so that the determined you can achieve what your intuitive voice is begging you to do. This is your life's mission. Don't shy away from it. Tell yourself you can do it. Right now. Because you can.

"God placed the best things in life, on the other side of fear"

– Will Smith.

CHAPTER 8
Weathering the Storm

Weathering the Storm

"And once the storm is over you won't remember how you made it through, how you managed to survive. You won't even be sure, in fact, whether the storm is really over. But one thing is certain. When you come out of the storm, you won't be the same person who walked in."

– Haruki Murakami

Disappointment. Devastation. Disillusionment. Despair. I could go on. These and other "d" words like them are immutable parts of life. Into every life a storm will appear. This is the part where you find out who you really are. In April of 2008, when I was 37 years old, and just a year after his nuptials, my best friend and brother passed away suddenly from a sparring accident. My older brother Anthony was the person I felt like understood me the most who wasn't also our mother. Losing my brother was a tragedy I was ill-prepared to handle. At the time, I had my own Kung Fu and Tai Chi school. I was training rigorously to test for 2nd Degree Black Belt. The last time I saw him out publicly, he was visiting my school for the first time. It was March of 2008. A couple of years passed by after his sudden death. I can't tell you anything about that time. It was a blur. Test came. I passed my test. Then I broke down. My grief spiraled out of control and I ended up closing my school of 86 students. I believe that is because while my mind (via my body) had a definite pursuit of preparing myself and my students to test, it shielded me from the true brunt of the pain. Once that cover was gone, I was exposed and vulnerable. It was two years later, but I took the hit of my brother's death like a Mike Tyson body blow. It was such a painfully devastating knockout punch. I closed my school and checked out of life. This began an arduous, sometimes surreal, ten-year process of grieving to heal.

Thank God I made it out of <u>that</u> storm. Thank God!

Have you ever had a disappointment that took you off course? A storm that came into your life? How do you condition your mind to take the hits and keep on ticking? We all know that life is unpredictable and volatile. We are literally living through a pandemic, as I prepare to publish this book. If your ship is strong enough, you can weather any storm. But, the vessel with no propulsion, or one that has a weight imbalance will be toppled by the crashing waves. And, if you're off-course you need a way to get back on the path. How do you steel yourself for the journey?

If you have your definite purpose, then it starts with the body. It goes to the mind. And then the spirit. Let me explain.

Your definite purpose is going to fuel you throughout the journey, but you need a few other things to make sure you get there. A homing beacon. A data center. And a GPS.

The **homing beacon** is your body. Your body is your engine and your temple. You have to build up your body so that it becomes a homing beacon for the frequencies needed to hear the messages your intuitive voice is working to send you. Once you start hearing, listening and acting on that voice, the messages will become clearer but only if you tune yourself to the right frequency. When you exercise, you feel better about yourself. You straighten your back and hold your head a little higher. It builds an amazing cache of confidence. We've talked about making sure that you take care of yourself, but I can't overstate how critical it is that this be an integral part of your plan. Your health is your wealth. Wealth is information. In other words, the more information you have the greater wealth you can build. It can't be just any kind of information though. It has to be worthwhile information. If you get yourself in shape, even as the process is occurring, you will increase your ability to recognize good info and act on it. You will also simultaneously align yourself with the best possible routes for that information to interact with you. Your confidence will grow exponentially.

The **data center** is your brain. Sure, we started with the brain. We'll finish with the brain, too. The brain is a muscle that you can exercise and make stronger. It is your computer server, hardware, software, wielder of will, and generator of drive. As you work to enhance the health of your physical body, it has a unique neurological effect on the brain. Synapses start popping. Memory receptors open. Blood flow to the brain increases. That frequency you are attuning your body for, finds its antennae and route in through your brain. If you're sending oxygenated red blood cells to the brain as with your breathing practice, you will maximize the power of your brain. Then use that power to reach your ultimate end goal, your definite purpose. We are unique in the animal kingdom in that humans can direct their brain to take them to whatever heights imaginable, and those yet unimagined. Dogs can only think about being dogs and fish can only eat, mate and swim. Our brain gets better with more exercise, both in the quality and in the execution of your thoughts and ideas. Like a gas tank, you have to feed it and fill it!

The GPS is your **Global Positioning Spirit**. Your spirit is your protector and your wings. Your spirit can take a bird's eye view and scout ahead, or it can push you through the most difficult situations. Your GPS also helps the right spirit, in the form of people that will help you achieve your definite purpose, to come into your life. If your GPS is sour or improperly tuned, it will ring wrong and untrue. People who could help or that would want to help will be repelled. Circumstances that would elevate your mission and windows of opportunity only you can see, will be blind and unavailable to you. You <u>must</u> manage your GPS. Again, you know people whose GPS is off or not functioning well. Be careful with them. Also, be careful not to give over control of your GPS to anyone. It can be easily hijacked and taken astray, pulling you with it. Guard your GPS with your life. You can cultivate and calibrate your GPS by meditating, praying, gardening, canoeing, or doing something you love that feeds your soul. For me, it's tai chi or baking or cooking. Once you get **your** GPS working at a bright, vibrant level, use it to shine your way forward in the darkness. Never take for granted the illuminating power of your GPS.

CHAPTER 9
If It's Possible, Then It's Real

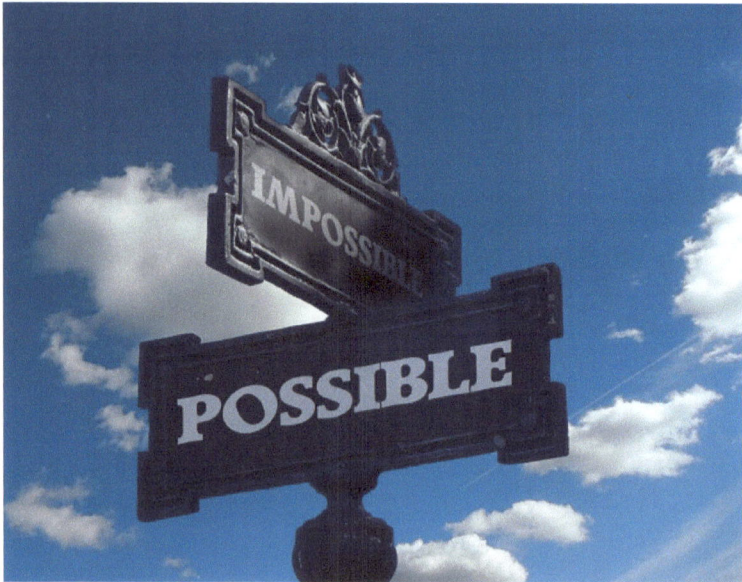

If It's Possible, Then It's Real

"Do or do not. There is no try."

- Yoda

The next thing we need to do to get your ship cutting through the water is work on your suspension of disbelief. Yes, your suspension of disbelief. You haven't done it, because you don't BELIEVE it's possible.

I love martial arts and tend to see and process things through a martial arts lens. I was talking with my young cousin Jabarri over a Christmas holiday break (he and his twin brother Kamau just graduated Morehouse), and he asked me what I thought about the more unbelievable things that you sometimes see happen in kung fu movies, like people walking on thin tree branches and jumping for way too long in the air, etc. Well, I said, I think it's just like believing in Superman or any other superhero. We know they can't actually fly, but we are undeniably inspired by their feats of superhuman strength, nonetheless. Whereas in Kung Fu movies at least the actors are, more often than not, good martial artists actually doing Kung Fu. I could go on and on with this analogy. And I don't mean to hurt your feelings if you love Superman or any other superhero. We all do. According to popular culture throughout history, the 'hero's journey' is a very well-known theme around the world.

But, in order to believe these characters, you have to believe in who they are and what they can do, like fly or pick up buildings. Put another way, you have to suspend your disbelief. Likewise, you have to stop telling yourself that you can't do it, and start telling yourself that you can. You have to start believing in the promise that is within you. After all, it's yours. You can believe in others' gifts, but not in your own? What manner of treachery is this? God has given you the ultimate tool and the means with which to put this tool to good use toward your exact powers. YOU **ARE** THE SUPERHERO. Now, please don't go trying to fly off a cliff or pick up a building. This is not a movie. It's real life. But, how are you not a superhero, figuratively speaking? How is it that we are enabled with such incredible gifts and immense power to pursue and achieve our definite end if we are not also somewhat super human?

Everything that you see and touch on a daily basis came from an idea. Your favorite restaurant. Your favorite app and the ones you don't like. Your car. Right now, you are thinking about them faster than I can write them. How is it that these things exist now? Think about when they didn't. How about the internet, for instance? Who could have predicted that the internet would exist or that it would be as widely used as it is today? New technological advancements are being made daily. New medical treatments are being developed daily. You can't tell me it isn't happening or doesn't exist, because we can both look at it together. It's tangible.

So, of course you say, well I can't see it, so it isn't real. Hmmm. Can you see the energy that causes "goose bumps"? No, you can't. But, you can see the results of this energy. Can you see air? No, but we breathe it all day every day. Your favorite new artist wasn't your favorite until you heard them, right? They weren't there before, but now they're as real as green grass.

The ideas that come to you are just as real. They will be tangible when you bring them forth from the regions of your mind that brought them to consciousness. If it comes to you as an idea, then it's possible. If it's possible, then it's real. And like Forrest Gump said, "that's all I have to say about that."

CHAPTER 10
Don't Give Up!

Don't Give Up!

We're starting to roll downhill now. This is the point in the program where I tell you to get mad as hell. Ok, maybe not that mad. But you have to get mad at the circumstances that you are unhappy with. You have to get mad at accepting mediocrity. You have to get mad at you brushing you off as if you don't matter. You have to start developing a "I won't give up" kind of mentality. A, "I won't accept loss as my destiny" disposition. We've already talked about how loss appears and can affect us. So, hear me clearly.

What I am saying is that you must start carrying with you a clause and covenant. A contract with yourself that says, I am no longer going to allow myself to cheat me. I will no longer be the pusher of my own demise. I will no longer be a spectator in my own life. A declaration of independence that says by the power of your sheer will and effort you will do whatever you need to do to achieve your definite purpose, and that nothing but God can stop you. Take your life back from floating along, to direct it with purpose. Some bodies of water have a pooling current where other floating boats will get caught and just go around in circles, sometimes colliding. Trust me. This is not where you want to be.

Make an announcement to yourself that this is a new day! And in this new day, you have decided to take the helm of your life and power your ship forward!! You are the captain. Announce to yourself that you and you have reconciled and that the scared you is welcome to enjoy the ride, but the determined and directed you is now steering! Be clear with yourself about where you fell into listlessness, and vow to never return. But, be sure to not waste time beating yourself up about how you got there. That is a misuse of your propulsion. Just keep looking to the horizon. There will still be storms, but don't worry. You know how to weather the storm. Your losses will become your victories. Say no more to "no", and yes to YOU because you are your best bet. In truth, you are your only bet. Just as with any muscle that you wish to develop, this too takes work and consistent effort. And you can do it. So, don't give up!

"Andre, this is Andre. Y'all is just gone have to make amends."

– Andre 3000

CHAPTER 11
Get to Know Your Bag

Get to Know Your Bag

The fresh thing to say these days is, "I'm in my bag", or "I'm getting to my bag." What does that even mean? I don't know, but I think it's a euphemism for getting money or getting to the money. Ok. But what really is in your bag?

In my opinion, it's not money. It's the means to the successful journey. And you won't get to the money without the means, or put simply, a plan.

You must plan your work and **work** your plan. It's your navigator. It's what will keep you moving toward the goal when you feel off-track. Don't be playful or coy about this. What is required is the work. You can have virtually anything you want if you are willing to put in the work necessary to achieve it. People are amazed when they see someone accomplishing big things or producing a lot of work in a short period of time. We tend to give them titles like, "The hardest working woman in show business", and "The hardest working man in broadcasting." There's "The Queen of Soul" and "The King of Hip-Hop". In sports, it's "The greatest of all time", etc.

Here's what I can tell you. Those folks didn't just stumble upon their uncanny success. They planned for it. Then after they planned for it, they worked their tails off. They made the plan work for them, even as they continued to work ON the plan (sometimes for years). They integrated the power of every turbine inside them to be directed into a singularly focused stream of consciousness that produced the results they sought. Then, and only then did they arrive at success. After the work.

If in your bag you have a defined set of tools no one else has, don't be surprised or afraid. We don't all get the same bag. Get to know yours. Get comfortable with your bag, because hidden in there is a gemstone. This gemstone is the key to creating and executing the plan that will bring the riches that we desire. To be clear, all riches aren't monetary. There will also be riches for the soul in your bag. All of it will help you determine your best route forward and keep you steaming ahead when rough seas or pandemics are at hand.

This is not for the faint of heart. You have to be a warrior! You have to be relentless about establishing your plan and working it. You have to be the captain of your soul. Keep in mind that a good captain always has a plan. Your bag is the key to your plan. It's time to work!

CHAPTER 12
Consistency

HELLO
my name is

CONSISTENCY

I MAKE IT HAPPEN DAY IN AND
DAY OUT. YOU MIGHT KNOW MY
GOOD FRIEND, SUCCESS...
WE'RE ALWAYS HANGING OUT!

Consistency

"Success isn't always about greatness. It's about consistency. Consistent hard work leads to success. Greatness will come."

– Dwayne "The Rock" Johnson

Are you about that life? Are you ready to get started? Is success something you believe can be yours? Or perhaps you are just fooling yourself. One thing is for certain. Everything that you have learned in this book has one magic key to unlock its true potential. That magic key is consistency.

Of all the chapters I've written for this book, this one was amongst the hardest. Here's where the mirror is right in front of you. You can pretend for other people and make claims that they can't easily verify. But for yourself? You can't easily lie to yourself. I mean you can, but you also know the truth.

How much work are you really putting in? Is your cheat meal day happening every other day? Are you working out 2-3 times per week? It's possible that you can get the results you want without being consistent, but only in an alternate universe. Here? This right here? This here is e'ry day necessary! Granted, you shouldn't do a 7 day per week workout regimen, at least at the beginning. That would be counterproductive. You must include days to rest and regenerate.

Even if you aren't working **out**, you should be working **toward** your plan with something that makes you better every day. Let me repeat that. **Get better every day**. Think of yourself like an old school model T engine. Or a turbine. You have to wind it up so that it gathers and stores enough energy to charge the machinery.

The way you cultivate that energy is by priming your engine on a daily basis. Whatever you have to do, do it. But don't let anything interfere with your consistent improvement. It's such a trip, that it feels like an out-of-body experience. You will look back after a short while and be amazed at the progress you have made. But don't stop to admire too long. You still have work to do!

The last CHAPTER
Move Your Ship!

Move Your Ship!

"You're gonna need a bigger boat!"

> – Roy Schneider as Brody, in "Jaws" (1975)

I hope this book has given you a clear understanding that you can't afford to be a floating boat. Floating along should be as scary a proposition for you as the one where you are in the open ocean with that lifesaver as your only means of survival. Not a good look.

You want great things for yourself and your family, right? Then, you must be willing and motivated to take control of your life. From now on, it is full speed ahead toward your definite purpose.

You can keep floating along through life, and you'll get nothing and like it! **Or,** you can decide to change your life for the better -- forever. Become your biggest fan. Be your own best mate. You deserve it! You are worth it! Wishing for success won't get you there, though.

You have to take action if you want results. You have to move your ship! And, you can. Set your plan and set sail. Don't worry if you get tired and have to stop for a break. Once you've rested, begin again and keep moving on the path toward your purpose. Now that you <u>know</u> you can...where will you go? Wherever you choose, your destiny awaits you.

I thank you for reading my book, **No More Floating Boats**©! I wish you the best possible life your boat can hold. Here's to you and your journey. Bon Voyage!

Far left: Sean sparring in the Shaolin-Do Fall 2007 tournament.

Direct left: Sean with 10th degree black belt, Shaolin-Do Grandmaster Sin Kwang The', and 8th degree black belt, Elder Master Joseph Schaefer (Aug 2007).

Sean C. Gooden, Sr., aka The Cookie

Anthony L. "Tony" Gooden

"The Sledgehammer" (Chocolate chocolate chip with macadamia nuts and cream cheese)

Boarding our boat!

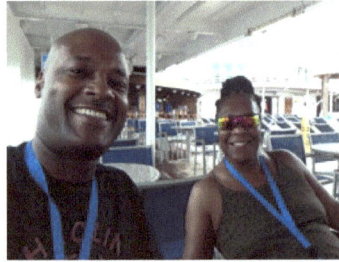

All aboard and ready to set sail.

Left: Mom surveys the landscape as we arrive in Nassau, Bahamas.
Below: Me at the back of the ship. I would work out here (w'o the chairs) after everyone went to sleep at night.

Right: White tip shark (about 7ft) at the Nassau Atlantis Aquarium.
Below: This 20ft high crystal greets you as you enter the Atlantis resort.

Left: The people and scenery of a street in downtown Nassau. Vibrant colors and bustling activity were everywhere.
Below: The penthouse suite at The Atlantis Resort. Reportedly, only $25,000 per night.

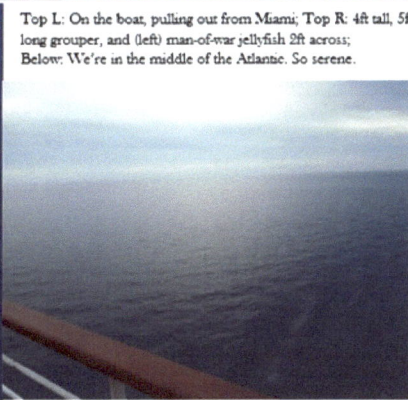

Top L: On the boat, pulling out from Miami; Top R: 4ft tall, 5ft long grouper, and (left) man-of-war jellyfish 2ft across; Below: We're in the middle of the Atlantic. So serene.

Left: One of our ports was at Halfmoon Cay in the Cayman Islands. Below: Turks Head Inn and Mansion historical plaque in Turks and

Below: We often stopped at private islands in the Cays to have beach days. Right: When you go to Turks and Caicos, make sure you get a real island tour. Our tour guide took us all over the island, including to see the Grand Turk Historic Lighthouse (lighthouse below).

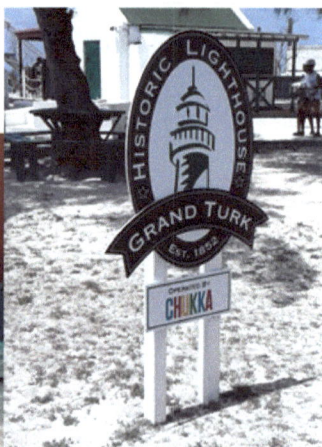

Below: On the boat, we created bonds to last a lifetime. One was with my brother, Dre', producer extraordinaire from Denver, who was on the cruise with his mother and fiancé'. We hung out tough, including during a tour of Turks and Caicos.

Bottom L (l-r): Mom, Rishia (Dre's fiancé'), Dre', Stacey (Dre's Mom), Me. Bottom R: Entrance to the Turks and Caicos Community College.

What are people saying about **No More Floating Boats?**

"Brilliantly written with easily applicable suggestions of what we need to do NOW to live our personal best journey in life. As we adjust to a new global normal, Sean Gooden has shared invaluable tools to help us navigate life on a more positive, satisfying and productive path, maximizing our innate abilities. The timing of this book could not be more perfect!"

-- Dr. Kirsten K. Shepard, LMT, DC

"Do you ever see that your pursuits are more haphazard than intentional? Do you procrastinate? Do you tumble into circumstances without a plan? Do you feel like your boat is listless and not getting you where you want to go? **No More Floating Boats** is a guidebook that will help you hear the intuitive voice inside you and will show you how to follow its guidance. In writing this guide, Sean cast an eye to the steps he's taken on his own pathway, and focusing on the lessons therein, he coalesced the significance of his choices and now he is lovingly sharing those lessons. **No More Floating Boats** will help readers draw on their inner peace to receive the energy that is there for seekers. This energy is a gift for you. Use it to program clarity of mind, define your purpose, and achieve your goals."

-- Dr. Carla Fjeld, PhD., Human Nutrition and Nutritional Biology

About the Author...

Sean C. Gooden, Sr., is the soon-to-be best-selling author of **No More Floating Boats**, a book dedicated to helping anyone reading it to find their path forward and move their ship, especially through the storms. Pain hurts. It can also bring clarity. It was the pain of the loss of Sean's older brother, Anthony, in 2008 that took him through the worst ten-year period of his life.

Usually a positive thinker, Sean lost hope for the future. His journey out of depression and back to a fruitful, fulfilling life came full circle on a real-life cruise, that became the metaphor for this book. Read it and find your path forward.

Sean currently teaches martial arts (kung fu and tai chi) and owns a gourmet cookie company (GoodenSweet Cookies) in his hometown of Austin, Texas. He is a 2nd degree black belt preparing for testing to 3rd degree black belt. He is the father of four children, and a grandfather.

www.ingramcontent.com/pod-product-compliance
Lightning Source LLC
Chambersburg PA
CBHW042107110426
42742CB00034BA/104